Literature written for young adults...

by young adults.

Allow yourself to be surprised.

Young Writers Anthology

Racing Toward Dawn

Derek Koehl and Tavares Stephens
Editors

VERBALEYZE
Press

Atlanta

Young Writers Anthology, Volume 1
Cover design by Derek Koehl
Editing by Derek Koehl and Tavares Stephens
ISBN: 978-0-9856451-0-6
Library of Congress Control Number: 2013938018

VerbalEyze Press books are available at special discounts for bulk purchases in the United States by corporations, institutions and other organizations.

For information, address VerbalEyze Press, 1376 Fairbanks Street SW, Atlanta, Georgia 30310.

VerbalEyze does not participate, endorse, or have any authority or responsibility concerning private correspondence between our authors and the public. All mail addressed to authors are forwarded, but the publisher cannot, unless specifically instructed by the author, give out an address or phone number.

VerbalEyze Press
A division of VerbalEyze, Inc.
www.verbaleyze.org

Table of Contents

Wendy Noreña

Trence King

Aly

Critical Reading Questions and Writing Exercises

Young Writers Anthology

Foreword

This edition of the *Young Writers Anthology* is a result of the vision that took shape four years ago. That vision—to foster, promote and support the development and professional growth of emerging young writers—is the guiding principle for everything we do at the VerbalEyze Writers Cooperative and through VerbalEyze Press. The *Young Writers Anthology* embodies two components of the VerbalEyze mission: one, to engage young people in and with creative writing and two, to provide talented young writers the opportunity to become published authors and learn the business aspects of being a professional writer.

Technology is transforming more than the mechanics of book publishing; we believe it enables a transformation of the very fabric of the publishing industry. VerbalEyze is working to bring the advantages of a new publishing approach to today's generation of young writers.

In addition to the craft of writing, we teach young people the business of writing and a revolutionary framework for writing and publishing that is fully cooperative. With the *Young Writers Anthology* and our innovative royalties model, we are enabling young writers to say, "I am my scholarship!"

We thank you for the support you have shown these young writers through the purchase of this anthology. *Racing Toward Dawn* brings you some of the most outstanding poetry and short stories by young writers whose middle school and high school ages stand in contrast to the power of their words and the depth of their vision into the human condition.

Allow yourself to be surprised. We did.

The Editors

Note to Educators

"Before one can think critically, one must be able to think creatively."

Fellow educator,

Whether you are a public or private school teacher, a home school teacher, or youth worker, our goals are the same: to engage the creative capacity latent in all our children and teach them to harness that capacity to bring about change in their own lives and in the world around them. *Young Writers Anthology: Racing Toward Dawn* is aligned with these objectives in two ways.

First and foremost, this anthology is literature written by young people. Engagement with the creative qualities of literature is instrumental to the process of awakening creativity in students. I believe this engagement is strengthened by the perception of shared experiences and perspectives that occurs when a reader identifies with a writer.

Second, the editorial team at VerbalEyze Press contains several members who are also professional educators. For each selection in the anthology we have provided a critical reading question and a writing prompt, all aligned with the Common Core State Standards. The critical reading questions help focus students on core thematic and analytical aspects of the selections. The writing prompts variously challenge students to write in explanatory, analytic and creative modes as they respond to or reflect on central ideas and concepts within each selection.

We have invested our energies into making the *Young Writers Anthology* a reality for one simple reason: we believe in young writers and young people. We are encouraged that you share that belief.

Derek Koehl, M.Ed.

Natalie Camrud

Because the Crow Flew South

Because the crow flew south
I flew north to visit you,
To eat apple pie while the bitter winds raged outside
And feign surprise at the red sweater you made.
I added it to my growing collection when I got home.

Because the crow flew south
I flew north to comfort you,
To hold your hand while you reminisced on the good days,
And dodge the tray you threw on the bad ones.

Because the crow flew south
I flew north to bury you,
I wore black instead of red,
And stood under the canopy as they lowered you into
The icy ground while the bitter winds raged inside.

Obsessed

I am obsessed with tattoos
And elephants,
Therefore it is fitting
That I shall be getting an elephant tattoo
On my thigh,
Someday.
Once I no longer live
With Brad and Marissa,
Fondly known as
Mom and Dad
(Not necessarily in that order)
In the meantime I stick with
The conventional obsessions,
Boys,
And the color pink

Things I Can Never Say to You

The first time you kissed me
I fell out of my chair;
Could you hear my heart beating, like a hummingbird's wings?
I was so far gone already,
I mistook your lust for love
And now I'm shattered,
Because when you said those three little words
You were thinking of steamy windows and stained sheets;
I was thinking of holding hands
And being able to cry on your shoulder.
And now,
I hate us,
And I hate you,
But no matter how hard I try baby
I just can't
Let you go

Elephant

If I were an elephant too,
I'd want you to cover me the way you do
When you think a comrade is dead,
With branches.
With leaves.
With breath.
I would eat silt and grass
Roaming the Savannah as the years pass
With you by my side.
Grey.
Solid.
Weathered.
We would walk in the sun
And then start to run
When we heard the safari coming,
Extravagant.
Massive.
Savage.
We would hide from their eyes
Because our dead brother still burns in our minds,
Just remember,
If I were an elephant,
I would
Never
Forget.

 **Natalie Camrud** has lived in Atlanta for most of her life. She discovered her passion for writing in her English class sophomore year, when her teacher assigned her first ever creative writing assignment. She loves to write because it is the only way for her to express everything that's on her mind. Natalie also enjoys painting and swimming. Natalie is currently the editor of her school's newspaper and plans to keep writing in college.

Emily Glenn

Backspace

Click click clack, click click.

The day outside is as colorless as the dreary sunlight that filters in through my window. Blurry mist hangs over the soggy brown grass, dead beneath a pitiful half-layer of slushy snow. Water drips halfheartedly in the gutter outside the window, clogged with rotting leaves that no one ever bothers to clean away. The sky lies obscured behind a roiling mass of foreboding clouds, and last time I checked, the weather-beaten thermometer in the kitchen window hovered just above thirty-six degrees Fahrenheit.

Click click, click... clack.

Clack, clack, pakpakpakpak.

My backspace key sounds different from the others on my keyboard.

It's shinier—the white label nearly burnished away by four years of lightning-fast fingers, writing and deleting and writing again.

Mostly deleting.

I glare suspiciously at the flashing black cursor at the end of the first line.

When it begins to annoy me after seventeen blinks, I slam the laptop shut and shove my chair back from my desk. I rise quickly, pacing across what I can find of my floor in feverish agitation.

Inspiration. I could strangle that minx.

Every time I think I've managed to get a grip on her and scramble back to my desk in ecstatic exhilaration, thinking I may finally be able to write something worthwhile, she darts just out of reach, cackling evilly and dancing away. My friends think I'm going insane. If words don't begin flowing soon, I may well be.

I trip over the corner of my dresser, barely managing to catch myself before crashing to the floor.

The room around me looks as though a tornado ripped through it; clothes, both fresh and unwashed, are strewn everywhere. Notebooks, pens, and torn sticky notes litter my desk. An iPod dock is buried beneath a mountain of junk, and my bed has resigned itself to being a disheveled mass of tangled blankets in the corner. It has every right—I spent last night in a sleepless turmoil, and I think the last time I emerged from my cave for more than five minutes was sometime last week.

I glance out the window and then back to my trashed room.

What a way to spend Christmas break—living like a hermit amid the depths of my room with no idea what the date is and empty Ski cans thrown all over. The outside world must think I've died.

I throw on one shoe, dig for the other, and brush off my coat. It's not five minutes before I'm striding out the door, slinging my messenger bag over my shoulder with one hand and struggling to button my coat with the other.

The frigid, dank December air smacks me in the face when I slam the front door behind me. It's freezing, stinging my stuffy nose, but even the cold isn't enough to cover the fishy stink; the mud here is disgusting. I make sure to keep to the sidewalk.

The winter world is dark. Damp and roiling clouds blot out the sky. A shiver shoots down my spine as a gust of frozen wind whips around me, and I quickly throw up my hood to shrink gratefully back into its warmth. But even as cars buzz by on the road beside me, spewing soggy gravel behind them, I feel happier than I have in weeks.

Winter is beautiful, assuming you're not stuck in southern Illinois.

Here you just have to make the best of it. At least the imagination to make it beautiful is a gift I possess, if I struggle hard enough to veil it behind twilight-misted glasses.

I'm not sure where I'm going. I'm not even sure what time it is, other than daytime; my watch was lost sometime yesterday to the rabid jaws of the mess in my closet. I swear, eventually strange, mangled creatures mutated by toxic waste will emerge from that door. At least they'll be well-fed.

My feet set off without me, but I can't bring myself to mind too much. I merely follow them with a mild sense of interest, hoping they don't decide to stub my toe again or run into a mud puddle and soak my shoes with fishy grit.

The walk into the heart of town isn't overly long, and the closer I get, the less puddles of slimy muck and jagged slabs of sidewalk there are to avoid. Just when I think I'm in the clear though, a tree thinks it funny to stretch a knobbly root right out in front of where my foot wants to go. I yelp—fall—jump back up again. My hands are scraped just enough to sting. I roll my eyes.

Yelping, falling, and jumping back up again have become far too routine for my liking.

The thought of using my beloved and loathed backspace key on my own clumsiness is intriguing.

I don't even bother attempting to snatch at the inspiration that begins to do the polka, as obnoxiously as possible, in taunting circles around my head.

I reach the town square, where the concrete of the sidewalk is pristine and white, and I still somehow manage to trip over my own feet at the crosswalk. A small smile quirks my chapped lips. The lights here are beautiful, but the fountain lies blank and dormant for the winter. It should be beautiful—all golden, glowing water and flowing mist, taking on a light and life of its own. In warmer months, I could spend hours sitting and watching it flow, writing my latest novel and retreating happily from reality.

Writing. I scowl down at my messenger bag, giving it a pointed smack. This is clearly all the fault of Backspace and his nasty little minion, Blinking Black Cursor.

I stand before the slumbering fountain, immersed in my thoughts. I catch sight of it.

A wide front window glows with soft, warm light against the depressed gray of the winter world around me, a name painted in beautiful golden script across the front window. *La Rose Noire.* I'm spellbound. It's French.

The cafe is beautiful. The start of inspiration takes root in the depths of my mind; it leaves me perplexed and mesmerized. How have I never caught sight of this strange, entrancing place before?

Without a backspace glance, I advance across the square and my clumsy, frozen hand takes hold of the cafe's old door handle. Against the soggy, ice-cold air of December, it is dry and warm. I am entranced. Pushing on the latch, I step inside.

The second my foot touches the shining wood floor, warmth surges through me, enfolding me like a cloak. The room is small, and beautiful—it's all so bright, so golden, that I smile in awe, looking around with wonder. I slip off my coat, walking over to a corner booth beside the window, and place it in the seat across from me. Seeing the letters on the window this closely only confirms my impression that they've been painted by a skilled, steady hand.

Behind the counter, the swinging door to the kitchen sways lightly, and a bouquet of dark roses sits in a cut-glass vase beside the cash register.

The door swings softly shut behind me, closing with a small click. I hardly notice. Inspiration has ceased her polka, in favor of practically hurling herself at my head, throwing arms around my neck and squeezing rather brutally hard.

I jump for my laptop, hastily open a new document, and watch in amazement as Blinking Black Cursor flies across the page.

* * * * *

I write all afternoon. By the time I close my laptop, letting my eyes fall shut and leaning back against the dark, soft leather of the booth behind me, an uncontrollable smile tugs at my lips, and I laugh in amazement. I don't know where that came from, but that's not even the tip of the iceberg; my mind is reeling with ideas, begging to be written, scrambling to shove each other out of the way and be the very first in line.

Suddenly, it strikes me that I didn't use Backspace once.

I open my eyes.

A warm, steaming mug of mocha coffee sits before me, half-gone, and I wrap my fingers around it cautiously. Sure enough, it is still the perfect temperature that it was when I noticed it sitting on the table an hour earlier. The kitchens' swinging door still moves slightly, but there has been no one to move in or out of it the entire time I have been sitting in this booth, and no draft to make it sway.

The window beside me should give off a cold aura, with the freezing air behind it. I place my hand on the glass; it is not even cool. Foreboding fingers scuttle down my spine as I suddenly notice that the lettering on the window, painted with such intricacy, is not backwards from the inside. I am certain that I read it perfectly from the outside, as well.

Most of all, in the deathly silence of the cafe, I finally realize that I am alone.

Now I shiver.

But despite my sudden foreboding of this place, with its warmth and quiet, and wonderful coffee, I smile as I slowly rise from my corner booth and slip my laptop back into my bag. I stand and look around, heading for the door, but stop with my fingers on the handle.

It doesn't feel right to leave without some sort of payment for the ideas flooding my mind, and of course, the delicious coffee. I pull a battered five dollars from my pocket, walk back over to the table of the corner booth, and place it beside the empty ceramic mug, my fingers hesitating lightly over the crumpled bill. Something prevents me from leaving it there.

I turn back to the cafe, taking it all in one last time before heading once more for the door. "*Merci*," I murmur, thinking of the glorious dormancy of Backspace and the way I have written today.

I will be back soon.

I step out into the December cold once again. It doesn't seem quite as fishy or dank as before, and the lingering warmth inside my coat brings a smile to my lips.

When I am halfway across the square, I cannot help myself; I look back over my shoulder, to find only a blank, dark storefront where *La Rose Noire* stood minutes before. It isn't a shock. I nearly laugh, shaking my head, before turning and continuing down the sidewalk.

I think of the dormancy of Backspace's havoc and pull up my hood as slowly, the cafe's warmth begins to fade.

Oh yes, I'll be back sometime soon.

 **Emily Glenn** is a writer and artist who lives in Highland, Illinois, with her parents and four cats. In third grade she was dubbed the Queen of Verbs; in fifth, she went to the state conference of the Illinois Young Authors' contest, and has been addicted to words ever since. When not wearing the letters off the keys of her laptop, she's commonly found on Tumblr, giggling at whatever she's reading, dabbling in the strange and somewhat creepy, or watching old black-and-white films. She's first chair flute in the middle school band, lives off of coffee and chocolate, and is absolutely obsessed with all things Marvel.

Isabel DeBre

Reflections on a Palm Desert Dinner Party

I.
it's the twilight of that final spring,
when the smog tastes darker—
in sullen valleys, gaunt like her daughter,
in vast California supermarkets, by the watermelons.

they live.
or, more specifically:
they watch people walk
with an inner peace,
and envy them.

II.
they squeeze through the screen door,
with *Coexist*, an Ojai wine,
exchange limp hands and
stand by the couch,
watch condensation stain a vase.

III.
she presses a tiny dog to her breasts,
"someone might as well feel them,"
she says,
her husband stares
out the window
at rocks, heaped in the dark backyard.

IV.
"All marriage is suffering,"
he says to the desert wind,
the night smells of cigarettes,
she
swallows smoke, and has nothing to say.

V.
They prefer to watch the palm trees
waving wildly,
shrouded in clay,
urging them
somewhere,
anywhere
but here.

VI.
On the drive home
the traffic is heavy and the hot wind blows
sand through the windows,

he sings,
and she listens,
but only because she knows Marvell well,
"The grave's a fine and private place,
but none, I think, do there
embrace."

VII.
when it's too dark to tell,
and she can sense thirty miles of
dust creeping through the door cracks,
she touches his leather seat,
and lets her fingers hang
—just for a moment on the seam.

because that is enough.

VIII.
in the distance,
a diesel stack warms and flutters,
and she watches,
knowing.

There is no other life.

Cambodian Nights

The cicadas scream.

She focuses on the sky. From the top of the hill, where the orphanage sits, she watches the gold lights veer and retract, the warm purple pigmenting and deepening and spreading. She breathes; the wind smells of sweet cigarettes. The rice fields in the distance tremble in yellow, glowing with the sun's blood.

She holds her breath until the first rip of pink burns into the dark. At home, in Los Angeles, pink is the color of fleshy watermelon at summer pool parties, of roses budding in her elementary school garden. But here, in Cambodia, pink is the color of roasting animal flesh, of crying children writhing in their sheets until dawn.

A group of orphans huddles on one edge of the parking lot, and she stands on the opposite end—a different axis of the world.

She can feel them glaring, giggling from across the gravel. They always giggle because she smells strange, like foreign linen. She glares back, her hand placed self-consciously on her hip.

At age twelve, she isn't used to this. The movies and books told her that not belonging would come later, in high school cafeterias. But the feeling runs through her now, like thread through a needle.

The door of the orphanage building drifts open with the wind. She can hear the deep voices of men and the scratching of stubble. Father is in there. She knows this. Her father is doing business with the owner of the orphanage, the sort of business she doesn't try to understand. He promised her that Cambodia would be a vacation, with tamarind juice in frosted glasses. But at the orphanage, only brown dust seeps from the faucets.

"It's a fine establishment," she hears her father say, his deep voice echoing from inside the building. "The white man's burden, eh?" and then her father laughs, the kind that starts in his belly.

She creeps through the front door. The children's voices vibrate through the wooden walls. They sing what must be silly jump-rope songs in another language. Inside, the walls are stained white, like in a hospital.

She tries to follow the voices, but the cicadas seem closer, screaming louder, drowning her father's conversation in their songs. They scream, *why are you here?* She does not know. Every morning, her father drives her to the orphanage, and they linger until dark. It's a strange feeling: to go somewhere and not know why, to ask questions that her father pretends not to hear. She knows she has been tricked, but she keeps hoping that her father will make a right turn one morning, drive onto a beach and buy her a popsicle that drips and stains the sides of her mouth. So she waits for hours and days. She sits on the curb of the parking lot, watching the sun move.

She walks closer to the door.

"I can't afford to feed them," says another voice. It must be the owner talking now. He wears shirts with floating cats on them, unbuttoned just enough to see the swirls of his chest hair. Whenever he looks at her, the girl feels uneasy, as if those Cambodian worms the doctors warned her about are crawling in her stomach.

"I'm practically bankrupt—"

"No one gives a damn," says her father.

She doesn't like to hear her father say damn. He only swears when the bedroom door closes and he yells at her mother.

"That's the thing about the third world. Regulations go out the window."

She leans against the wall of the room to listen. The wood moans. Her father flings open the door.

"What are you doing here?"

"You took me here. Remember?" she says, and closes her eyes so she won't cry.

"This is business talk." He raises his voice and speaks slowly, like the way he talks to foreigners. "This is not child talk."

She knows it isn't child talk, but nothing these days is child talk, especially not the conversations in offices or bedrooms. Especially not the conversations about the orphanage. These conversations make her mother sick. Sad, her mother says, but mostly sick. When the girl leaves for the orphanage with her father in the morning, her mother stays locked inside the hotel room. She lies there all day on the unmade bed, staring at the ceiling fan. Last night, when it was dark and her father was drinking in the lobby, she curled inside her mother—inside the warm gap that was once the womb.

"I can't stand to see the children," her mother whimpered, rustling the girl's hair. "Your father used to be a good man."

Now her father is closing the office door. "Ask the cook for dinner," he says.

On any other night, the girl would have left. She would have walked down the hall into the kitchen with its dark, crunchy food. She would have closed her eyes and swallowed the crickets—pretended they were not crickets, not the creatures that crawled up her shower drain on Sunday afternoons back in Los Angeles.

She tries to walk down the hall, but fragments of voices and pictures settle strangely in her bones. She feels her mother's vomit in the bathroom and the hushed arguments behind doors and her father's shouts—his red face. Her father turns red only when he means it. It gives him away even before his hands. And so the girl decides not to leave, instead to press her ear against the wall like in those spy games she used to play when she was little and wondered if her next-door neighbor was a murderer. Voices move through the wood like water.

"I can pay you," her father says. "I can help you. Why do you think I brought my goddamn family here in the first place? I'm willing to move here. But I need a return."

There is some shuffling and mumbling.

"What do you want?" the owner asks, his voice trembling.

"I have nothing—"

"Make them work." It is her father's voice again, this time louder—the red on his face bleeding into his throat. Outside the children scream. It must be a snail. They always scream when they see snails. "The children can work in sweatshops, or whatever. I don't care."

"We can't afford to pay…"

"Exactly." It sounds like her father, but something caught in his voice makes her want to check again. "Don't you get it? Third world…no regulations…."

A crash in the sky shakes the windows. The voices stop. Something shatters again, and she feels the echoes of the sound in the trees and in her stomach. It is like fireworks, except when she peers through the hall window there are no colors. Just darkness. Someone screams. It is a very particular scream—very feminine, like the opera. It must be a large snail. Her father says damn again, except this time he yells it. The door opens, and her father tells her not to move. His face is red. He and the owner rush outside.

Her toes hurt from looking out the window. She hears motorcycle wheels twisting in the dirt. She hears crying. Who is crying?

She feels the sounds crackle inside of her, like static. She moves through the hall and into the night. Something turns inside her stomach.

The cicadas' sirens cut through the wind. She stumbles over a large rock, crashing into the gravel. Her knees are bleeding; she knows this, but she can't feel anything, as if she is no longer attached to her own body.

Sprawled over the ground, she looks up at the sky. Its pink has faded. She pushes away the rock that tripped her, but it won't move. She pushes harder, and then she stops because the rock is warm, faintly pulsing, with an arm, and a foot, and a sandal.

She pulls the limbs closer; so close that this boy is almost inside of her. She does not know his name because she has never asked. His hand falls over her hip. Together, in the dark, they are anonymous. She can smell the death around her, but somehow, she feels herself buzzing—alive.

Her father calls her name. She does not respond.

The boy mumbles something into the dark space between their skin.

The cicadas scream.

"I'm here," she answers.

 Throughout high school, **Isabel DeBre** has been writing fiction and poetry. She attended the New England Young Writers' Conference at Bread Loaf, the Kenyon Review Young Writers' Workshop, and will be attending the Iowa Young Writers' Studio summer 2013. Her short fiction and poetry has been published in several literary journals, and this year she received a Scholastic Art and Writing Gold Key for a short story. For the past three years, she has been writing articles on human rights issues for Care2.com, a website that spreads awareness about social justice causes.

Hayden Kinney

The Fall

I tap the top of my steering wheel three times before I start my engine. I know I'm not going to die in a car accident because I tapped the top of the wheel three times. Parked in my driveway, I pull a postcard from my pocket. On the front is a man with bronze mechanical wings standing on the ledge of his apartment window. You can't tell how far up he is. You can only see a few stories in the middle of the neighboring buildings; because of this it has the effect of making you feel as though you are the man at the ledge, but unlike him, you can't look down and tell how far you will fall if your constructed wings fail. I flip the postcard over, there's nothing on the other side. The person who bought it probably didn't have anything to say. They just wanted the picture. I back the car out of the driveway and out into the street, the newly paved street that curls and turns past the houses like a smooth black snake, gliding into some dark crevice in the dense black horizon.

I'm going to the fair tonight. It's summer after all, and it seems like the right thing to do. Faith, my girlfriend, is going to be there, so that's a plus. I figure that nights where I kiss someone are better than the nights I don't. If I flip on my high beams three times I'll go to second base tonight. I shouldn't because this is just perpetrating my crippling OCD or something like it, but I do it anyway: *click on, click off . . . click on, click off . . . click on, click off.*

At a stop sign I look over to my right where there are two homeless people on a bench. The man, a frazzled grey beard with a bright blue beanie, is being kissed all over by a woman with electric mud-brown hair and a Mickey Mouse sweater that is probably older than I am. She's folded on top of him like beach chair.

I tried to think if there was anytime I had done that with Faith. We have only been dating for a couple weeks. We kissed briefly once, after a date where at her doorstep we had stood around mumbling small talk and goodbyes for a minute and eventually exchanged a brief lip-press which made me feel similar to when I was paired up with girls for PE dance; it was quick, awkward and impersonal. It didn't bother me at the time that much though. I had figured that's what these things are like anyway, but now it makes me feel uncomfortable. I start drumming my fingers against the emergency brake.

I realize I've been at the stop sign for about a minute and quickly jerk my foot off the brake and drift across the intersection, relieved that no one had noticed me. Not even the homeless couple, two mangy cats licking each other's wounds. It must be nice to have someone lick your wounds for you, get the spaces you can't reach. I don't mean that in a weird way or a sexual way but more in a spiritual way I guess.

As I'm driving along, the streetlights, they remind me of clock hands marking off my time. Each look the same, and each fall to the wayside at the same rate as the others. I close my eyes and count to ten. I'm annoyed at myself for doing this, but it makes me feel less tense.

As my eyes close I recall a dream I've been having recently. In the dream I'm crossing a bridge, but about halfway across I fall off, and the thing is I sort of do it on purpose. I fall and break both my legs, landing in a hospital. Two nurses pick me up; one looks like Faith, and the other one looks like my mom, and they are both the exact same height. The nurses put me in the bed and give me anesthesia so that they can set my bones, but it doesn't work. I keep trying to fall into an artificial coma, but I can never quite do it. I look where they put the needle. A thin trail of blood slithers down my forearm like a crimson snake.

A couple loud bumps are followed by a cracking noise, and I've driven straight onto the sidewalk and rolled over someone's white picket fence.

You can't tap your way out of this one, I think.

My first reaction is to put the car into reverse and quietly drive away. Nobody noticed me at the stop sign so maybe my luck will hold. A man opens the door and steps onto the front porch.

"What the hell is this?"

"I'm really sorry. I think I might've hit your fence. I don't know—"

"You think?"

I again consider shifting to that big R and slamming on the gas, but no, I've already acknowledged this. Too late now for any tricks.

"Come inside, we'll discuss this over some tea. You like tea?"

"Uhh . . . sure."

I put my car into park on his front lawn and walk inside. I tap my car roof three times so he won't murder me with a blender. Inside his house, nothing stands out except for an empty birdcage hanging in the entryway.

"What's your name kid?"

"Tom."

"Mine's Elijah."

We shake hands; his feel like they had scales like a reptile or a bird.

"Why'd you hit my fence?"

"I don't know. I'm just tired I guess"

"Well then the tea'll do you good."

He might be the lankiest person I've ever seen. He's not even that tall, but every part of him seems like it's been artificially stretched. He comes back and hands me my tea.

"What do you want to do with your life?" he inquires in a

gruff tone.

"Huh? I don't know; go to college I guess at this point."

"What's your passion though? What do you do that gets you excited every morning?"

"I dunno. I like math alright I guess."

"Jesus," he exhales and glances over to the birdcage on his right briefly before returning to me. "Where were you headed?"

"To the fair. My girlfriend's waiting for me there."

"That's cute. You've got a girl."

"Yeah, I guess." I'm starting to feel wobbly, as if the room is balancing on a single tip and is teetering all around.

"Do you love her?"

"I—"

"She has your mother's eyes doesn't she?"

I'm shaking all over now. I'm teetering as if I was on some ledge even though I'm firmly planted on the wooden floor.

"Of course you don't know your mother. You might not even know what her eyes look like. She died having you. Isn't that right?"

He smirks and raises his eyebrows like he is a movie villain. In one swift motion he grabs me by the arm and drags me like suitcase. He pulls me through a doorway into a room. Even though it's pitch dark I see patterns of light dancing all around.

We stop, he pushes me, and I fall into a pitch-black pit. I wait to hit the bottom, but I don't. I don't think there is a bottom. I'd rather hit the bottom; at least things would make more sense. Instead I'm floating in utter nothingness. I open my arms like a bird, birds, birds are just reptiles with wings. They slither across the sky. I see a blood red cardinal flying above me. I don't know how I see it in the darkness, but I do anyway. I'm not questioning things right now.

I keep falling. Actually at this point I can't tell if I'm falling or ascending. I'm just moving. I see the moon. There shouldn't be a moon. There was no moon earlier tonight, but there it is, glowing like an angel.

I wake up, and I'm soaking wet. I slowly sit up. It's daytime, and I'm in the backseat of a car, backseat of my car. I'm no longer on Elijah's lawn, in fact I'm in my own driveway. As I'm grabbing for the phone in my pocket I feel something else there as well. I fish it out. It's a tiny wooden bird, a cardinal. It appears to be smirking but not with it's mouth, more with it's eyes like the Mona Lisa and glowing like the moon.

9/21/12

I have consumed the universe
In cosmic fruit
And found grand cities
Dissipate into empty foundations
For these towers were made not of

Concrete, but of snakes and vines
Wrapping about each other
And scaling towards
The heavens like skinny moths
To a warm light

And the sweet vibrations
Could no longer quench
My hunger for gleaming light it's
Nectar to fill my empty body
For they to, were hollow like dead trees

I consulted the
Frost coating my lawns and trees
It said to get lost in the woods
So that I could try to find my way out
Traveling along mysterious roads to strange worlds

Violent waterfalls which
Crash like dueling galaxies,
An entrancing war
With water and rock beating against each other
Like lovers entangled in lustful battle

There is a ladder
One of firm solid wood
That could be climbed
To the virgin crevices of
The dense, dark blanket of reality

I wrap my soft palms around one rung
Feeling the cold golden wood
And deciding it is not for me,
Wander towards the endless forest

Towards giant trees of the west
Solid and sedentary
I walk between and beneath them
Setting off on my rambling journey

 **Hayden Kinney** grew up in the San Francisco Bay Area in Marin County. He is a member of the Sonoma Academy High School Class of 2013 and Reed College Class of 2017. Hayden has concentrated on writing prose and poetry since he was 17 and hopes to continue writing long into the future.

Artistically he is inspired by various works of James Joyce, F. Scott Fitzgerald, Kurt Vonnegut, Hunter S. Thompson, Robert Frost, Allen Ginsberg, e.e. cummings, as well as the films of Jim Jarmusch, Alfred Hitchcock, Joel and Ethan Coen and Francis Ford Coppola.

Briana Richardson

Silence

Shhhh… Don't speak.
Just listen to my voice
And pay close attention to my words.
The things that I tell you
Are only for us to know,
They are true and last forever,
And they are not for show.
They will not be told
In the way you would imagine,
I will not talk, I will not speak,
Just listen to the silence.
Listen to the wind
And the things that pass right by you.
Listen to the air I breathe
And let it flow right through.
The silence that you hear
Is louder than my voice
It can only be heard if you listen,
It can only be heard by choice.
It tells the things I think

It shows just how I feel,
Words will not explain,
Because the silence is more real.
If you cannot hear it
Then you think it is not there,
It's not that you're not listening
It's because you do not care.
You do not want to listen
You do not want to know,
The feelings I can't express
The ones I cannot show.
The silence tells it all
Every feeling and every thought;
I cannot show you how to listen,
The lesson cannot be taught.
Just stop and listen to the silence
And maybe you will hear,
Everything I held inside
And all the things that were not clear.

Briana Richardson

Nothing

I'm standing in a field,
Of nothing and everything,
But nothing means a thing to me
If everything stays the same;
Nothing can hurt more
Than losing everything,
Everything could be given to me
But all of it means nothing;
If all the things
I knew were different,
And nothing was what I thought,
Then anything I
Thought could last,
Would die right in its spot;
Dead and gone
Never to return,
A scar left
From a burn;
A blur in my mind
A memory I forgot;
A mirage so tiny
And too small to jot;
Pictures fade
And pasts disappear,
The thoughts I lost
The captions clear.

Walking Backwards

I guess walking forward
Just doesn't come naturally
For me because
I often notice myself
Walking backwards again;
Taking steps into my past,
Remembering what went wrong,
Things never seemed to last,
At least, not for too long;
Ups and downs,
Rises and falls,
Trying to walk forward
But running backwards
And crashing into the wall.
Today, of course,
Is no different;
Pushing back emotions
And hiding what
I hope to cover,
My eyes will never open
To truths I couldn't see,
My mouth would never tell,
Secrets you shared with me.

I will never forget,
Lessons that I learned,
My heart would never heal,
Bruised. Battered. Burned.

When Reality Hits

I gave up on perfect

Because I am me
And regardless of what you see
I am reality.
I do not live
In dreams and fantasies,
Or aspire to things
That just cannot be.
Impossibilities,
Are like imperfections;
They are not a question,
They are answers
To what could be.
But who's listening?
No one cares about the truth,
They just see what society thinks.
They don't understand
What's at hand
And the power
That they hold,
But truth be told,
Everything will
Eventually unfold.
When they realize

That their pride
Has a price,
And they reap
What they sow,
But who knows?
Maybe their true colors
Will be revealed.
Maybe the truth
Will show them
What's really inside;
Maybe it'll show
What they tried to hide.
Maybe when things get hard,
They'll realize
That they shouldn't have
Given up their lives
From the start;
Becoming what they're not
Just to get to the top.
But it's a push.
All they ever needed was a fall,
For instance, when they realize that
What they've become was
Their entire fault;
Then their life
Comes to a halt,
But pause.
They rewind

And realize
Everything they left behind,
And fast forward
To see they were
Moving too fast
Toward a place
No one really
Wanted to be,
And they've become
Someone they didn't want to be,
But stop.
This is when it hits them.
This is when
It falls into place
And they realize
That all this time,
They've been
Floating in space;
And it hits them.
It hits them
Dead in the face;
And after all this time
They realize they've
Been mesmerized;
Tricked and conflicted
With tricks and conflicts,
And they quit.
They give up the lives

Briana Richardson

That were never theirs,
And right there,
People realize
That life isn't fair.

That's why I gave up.

I gave up
What people think,
Because before
I can blink,
They begin
To sink.
Drowning in
False hopes and dreams,
So I stop dreaming
False hopes
And false things
And wake up
To what reality
Really is.

Break the Glass

Tap on my window
'til you
Break down the glass;
Hold on to me
Close and
Make these moments last;
Kiss me on the
Cheek and
Never let me go;
Tell me all the
Secrets that
Only we know;
Promise me
Things that
Make me want you more;
Wrap me with arms
I've longed for;
Love me on
Days that
Never have an end;
Heal the scars
And the wounds,
Promise this won't end;
Whisper in the wind

Briana Richardson

Things you wish
Could be;
Tell them to my
Heart as

Promises to me.

A Monster's Victory

So you've got a
Knife in one hand
My heart in the other,
The two were never
Meant to
Be together, but you keep
Forcing them to
Mix like an
Abusive lover;
You never meant
To hurt but
You place the knife
Where you
Should be,
Filling the space
Between you
And me;
You bruised
My heart then
Patched the tears,
But you never
Seemed to
Be aware
That you
Were falling

To shreds and could
Never notice it
In the tears
You bled;
You never noticed how
Deep you
Cut your own scars,
Beating your own
Bruises with
Metal bars;
You picked
At your scabs
'Til your
Skin turned black,
You tried to hide
What you didn't
Want to show,
But I could tell by
How you crumbled,
You would
Shrivel then shrink,
I could tell
By how
You hid from
Things I would think,
You had always been afraid of
The truth,
You knew it would

Haunt you;
You couldn't stand the
Beating of rain
Against a window
Pane's portrait,
You could see
The nightmares
Coming alive,
Starting a riot,
You could see
The flame inside
Your heart
Burning within it,
But you
Couldn't stop.
You continued
To beat both
Of our sores
'Til they were
Bleeding to
The core,
But you could
Never see that
Something was wrong,
Your knife
Was singing
A monster's song,
And it was victorious.

Briana Richardson

Singing this
Song of victory,
This song that
Battered you
And me,
This song that
You should
Never sing,
But it's become
A habitual thing;
A song that
I will never sing,
A song that
Only monsters sing.

My name is **Briana Richardson**. I am a junior in high school. I was born and raised in Georgia, and I have been writing poetry since the 5th grade. I'm not exactly sure what inspired me start writing, but I never stopped. Poetry has always been something I loved, and it has opened my eyes to many different people's experiences.

For me, poetry has always been a form of release and has allowed me to express myself in ways I sometimes cannot do without it. I love poetry because it is very moving and inspires me to do better. I always strive to make myself better, and my poetry is how I encourage myself and others. When I write, it's not just for me but for others so that they can learn from poetry as I do.

Cristianna Cummings

Helena the Poet

"Frost crackles beneath my toes; stinging wind cools my nose; birds fluttering fills the sky; a loon sends out a mournful cry."

Helena giggled to herself with pleasure. She scribbled the rhyme down in her leather bound poem book before she forgot it. Stretching out her neck toward the sun and away from her scratchy wool scarf, she let the wind blow her luscious hazelnut brown hair behind her in a crazy dance.

"Helenaaaaaa," a voice from far away called.

"Coming!" she shouted back.

After glancing once more at the frost covered mountain lake, she ran toward the steep snowy hill where she had left her metal framed sled. Kicking the snow up behind her in powdery fluffs, she hopped on, flying down the hill in ecstasy. She stopped near a large pair of black button-up boots similar to her own. It was Miss Amanda, her tutor.

"Now Helena, hurry! I have been waiting nigh ten minutes for you. You're late for tea. The Pastor and his wife have come to visit. Lord knows how often they come. Your mother has worked herself into a tizzy," she said mostly talking to herself.

"You can't go in looking like a little hoodlum with your hair all blown around. Don't dawdle," she added as Helena stopped to pick up her fluffy tabby kitten.

"Yes, Miss Amanda," sighed Helena as they walked through the sleepy town toward home. Writing would have to wait 'til after tea.

~~~~~~~~~~~~   ~~~~~~~~~~~~

Ugh! What dreadfully boring people. The Pastor talked on and on about politics and high prices in the same monotone voice that made his sermons so unbearable. Couldn't they talk about something interesting, Helena brooded. Something like the pot-luck lunch this Sunday or the rumor of a poetry contest that had been circulating around town.

Helena despised having tea. For starters, it tasted horrible, like soaked rose petals. (Helena knew this because she had tried to make her own tea to impress her mother. It had tasted terri-ble.) Second of all, it seemed like such a waste of time when one could be doing much more interesting things like writing poems about her comical kitten or drawing a picture of a blue jay, for she was very fond of birds. But her mother thought tea a very proper practice and that the younger generation should learn such useful things, so Helena was forced to suffer through it.

Usually Helena could bear tea if she put three or four lumps of sugar in her cup. Once Mother caught her putting all that sugar in and scolded her. It was not lady-like, and further more she was not to do it anymore.

Helena hid a grimace behind the rim of her cup, partly from the bitter tea and partly from being bored to death. Pas-tor's monologue had moved to crops and, "did you think that this would be a good year for corn?"

"I am sure I wouldn't know," Mother replied. Thankfully, Pastor's wife took advantage of the small window of silence before her husband could start on another subject and said, "I am sure that your daughter," she gestured to Helena, "tires of our conver-sation. Hardly the thing little girls enjoy. Wouldn't you like to go play, dear?" she asked directing the question to Helena.

"Oh, very much. Thank you," Helena said desperate to leave. She glanced toward Mother for approval. But Mother was otherwise distracted, asking Matilda to bring in some more cakes for "our beloved Pastor."

Taking advantage of the situation, Helena curtsied to Pastor and his wife, snatched a delicate pink cupcake from Matilda (before Pastor could eat them all), and hurried off to the kitchen. Helena thought Pastor must have had quite a lot of tea and cakes in his life, for he had a large appetite as evidenced by a rather large belly.

~~~~~~~~~~~~   ~~~~~~~~~~~~

Helena was an only child, so as a consequence she was good friends with the maids and cook. As she went through the swinging doors that led into the kitchen, Vellma the cook looked up from violently stirring something in a red bowl.

"Don't spoil your supper. We'll be eatin' in an hour or so."

Helena sighed. She was always lectured not to spoil her dinner. She had seen one of her school mates eat a whole box of chocolates just before dinner, and he hadn't spoiled his dinner. He had eaten three helpings of mashed potatoes and chicken, ignoring of course the vegetables, pushing them to the side of his plate.

"Helena!" Vellma said sharply. "Stop day-dreaming and snap those beans for me! Your mother plans to cajole the Pastor and his wife into staying for supper, I 'spect."

"Yes, Vellma," Helena replied, reaching for the silver bucket filled to the brim with dark green beans. Helena never minded helping Vellma, even though she had a sharp tongue. She especially enjoyed helping when Vellma was making coffee apple cake. Helena could tell this was the case today because Vellma only used the red mixing bowl when she was making coffee apple cake. Everyone agreed that she made the best tasting cakes in the county, and possibly the whole world.

She was also known to withhold cake from people she was on bad terms with. Even Pastor knew about Vellma's cakes and was always extra polite when she was around.

Helena brought the bucket of beans closer to the kitchen door, straining to hear if their guests' conversation would be of interest to her.

"Oh, but Pastor, it would give me such great pleasure if you were to stay for dinner."

"We really couldn't impose," Pastor said as if he didn't want to be rude but at the same time not wanting to appear too eager to stay.

"Not at all," Mother replied pleasantly, "and I am sure you will want to stay for Vellma's fabulous cake afterward."

Helena couldn't hear Pastor's reply because just at that moment Vellma—swinging her cooking spoon in the air for emphasis—said, "Child, you shouldn't listen in on other people talkin'. It's rude."

Helena, not wanting to be on Vellma's bad side, reluctantly moved over to the stove where she could best smell the baking cake.

~~~~~~~~~~~~   ~~~~~~~~~~~~

To no one's surprise, and to Mother's delight, Pastor and his wife stayed for dinner. But dinner with Pastor took an extra long time because he kept up such a constant stream of chatter while he ate. Helena almost let out a sigh of relief when he finally stopped to eat his now cold beans.

After Matilda had cleared the plates, Vellma brought out the cake already cut into slices and placed on the fancy china. If Vellma hadn't done that Pastor would have eaten at least half, and there would have been nothing left for tomorrow's potluck.

"Oh my! Doesn't that look wonderful?" Pastor's wife said to no one in particular.

"Coffee apple cake!" Pastor exclaimed. "My favorite."

"I am so glad," Mother said. She was always happy when people enjoyed dining with them. In no time at all, the pieces of cake were devoured. Pastor hinted that he might like another piece, and Mother immediately asked Vellma to get the Pastor some more cake. Vellma brought the piece but withered Pastor with such a glare he didn't hint for any more after that.

Soon after, Pastor's wife decided it was time to take their leave and thanked Mother for the wonderful tea and dinner. As they were putting on their coats, the topic Helena had been waiting for finally came up.

Pastor's wife and Mother were talking about the Sunday potluck when Pastor's wife mentioned the church was holding a young writers poetry competition during the potluck. She noticed Helena was often writing things down in a little book and asked if Mother would give consent for Helena to enter. There would be a prize at the end, and the poem would be printed in the newspaper.

Helena's hopes soared; here was her chance to become a known author, even if it was only in the local newspaper for a few days.

"Certainly not!" Mother replied indignantly, crashing Helena's hopes to the ground. "That is such an unladylike practice, if you don't mind me saying," she said turning her nose up and giving a little sniff. "Thank you though for offering. I am sure there will be enough people to enter your contest without my Helena."

Helena could tell Pastor's wife was insulted. She stiffly thanked Mother again and quickly walked out the door onto the street with Pastor trailing behind.

Mother also seemed a little put off, but she didn't say anything. She simply stalked over to her sewing in the living room. Helena ran into her room, an idea forming in her mind. She could still enter the contest, anonymously. She flipped through her poem book and found one of her best:

A Light

You see a light far ahead;

the darkness around you is filled with dread.
You're drawn to the terrific light, but you know the darkness will
put up a fight.
Is the fight worth the light?
Yes, don't stay in despair: go to the light, and it will be there.

Helena thought that this one was her best, although it
didn't seem appropriate for Sunday church. She flipped through a
few more pages and found this:

A New Day

"It's a new day," I rise and say.
I may play the dawn to dark away.
A new start! A fresh heart! Beauty all around!
"Let us not waste time away."
Not clouds or rain or anything gray will spoil my ray of joy.
The sun shines.
My heart prays tomorrow will be as lovely.

"It's perfect," Helena thought. Fun and just right for church.
Helena copied the poem onto her best stationary with her best
handwriting. If she won, everyone could read it in the newspaper.
Helena was so excited that it seemed like hours before she finally
fell asleep.

~~~~~~~~~~~~   ~~~~~~~~~~~~

Sunday morning arrived; it was time for the contest. Hel-
ena was so excited she could scarcely eat her breakfast. Not that it
mattered much, the potluck would surely have a lot of food. The
church service seemed extra long that morning, and there was a
lot of fidgeting going on. After forever, the service ended, and it
was time to submit the poems. The judge would read them during
the potluck.

Watching Mother's imposing figure carefully out of the corner of her eye, Helena eased her way towards the big wooden box where contestants were crowding around to enter their work. After glancing around one more time at Mother, who was talking to Mrs. Fillmore, she casually dropped her slip of paper into the box with a trembling hand.

There was so much food on the tables inside the church that Helena didn't know where to begin. But that was not the case with Pastor; he went straight for Vellma's left over cake, starting the potluck off.

The ladies of Brunsburry certainly put all they had into a potluck. There were cakes and pies, turkey, mashed potatoes, breads and puddings, and lots of roast lamb with chestnuts. Someone even brought ice cream, which quickly disappeared.

After the potluck was devoured and the last crumb licked up, it was time to announce the winner of the poetry contest. As they waited for the judge to walk out, Mother made a snide comment under her breath to Helena, "Another word for poet is a lazy person who doesn't want to start their life."

Helena winced. Those words cut into her very soul.

Finally the judge (a well-known local poet) stood at the pulpit. "This was a very hard decision, so hard in fact that I couldn't pick a winner."

There was a collective groan from the poetry contestants.

"But," he continued, "I have picked the two best. One of them is a poem entitled 'The Shining Lake' by Randy Stuart. The other winning poem has been left anonymous but is entitled 'A New Day.' Congratulations to both! I have decided that the winners will be able to take an extra poetry class under my tutelage after school, if they choose to continue writing. Thank you for all your wonderful entries. Best to you for next year."

There was much applause. Randy was patted numerous times on the back. But no one was more ecstatic then Helena. She wanted to jump and shout; her happiness over flowing.

"A lot of vulgar nonsense," Helena heard Mother say, "for two children to win this poetry contest. As if one wasn't bad enough. If it were my child who had written anonymously I would give them a good switching." She looked sideways at Helena.

Helena suppressed a giggle as the people closest to Mother moved away from her. If only Mother knew. Helena's spirits would not be dampened however. She was a writer, and right now that was all that mattered.

 **Cristianna Cummings** lives in Loon Lake, WA with her three sisters—two of whom have been in a book recently—and one white fluffy dog named Marty. She enjoys writing poetry and short stories about things that inspire her.

"Helena the Poet" was inspired by Cristi's own love of poetry and of old-fashion style writing. She also wants to thank her mother for putting such an effort into helping her create this story.

Wendy Noreña

Somethingdoesntfeelrightwheni-
walkaroundhereanymore

One time I read
about a group called
the battle of the angels

They were resistors.
They resisted pain
And death
murder. Folly.
And they resisted living in a world
where these images are still
televised
but the revolution doesn't seem to have
arrived.

Maybe if the world
knew that there are more than enough
grains of wheat numerous as
grains of sand trapped between vacation maps
stored in car dashboards

to feed those infamous starving children in Africa
that everyone speaks of
as ghost images
radiating without consequence through pop
culture references
then maybe McDonald's could renounce it's golden arches
and show us
arches of light.

And if the world
knew how much money was really costing us
right now
at this moment
green streams
turning into rivers of
blood and broken tv parts,
and
unsafe neighborhoods
and sometimes the souls
of people we never expected,
but especially children who want
Barbie dolls instead of
voyages to see the most
beautiful parts of their
ancestral blood
then maybe we wouldn't inherit 100 acres of
our father's property
deeds

and still call this stolen land
a blessing.

If
the world knew
that there is
love

That hasn't been discovered
but will be dug up on hands and knees
with sand sculpture shovels
revealing lovers with limbs intertwined
a very testament
to the irrelevance of time
and the nature of burying that which
scares us and will later
put us under

Maybe then I could fly
across a thousand oceans
to see what once was
my small-tribe family
riding in the passenger seat of the plane with a cigar
chatting to the pilot
for free
because I can't afford to go on
the missions of reconciliation

that everyone wants to go on
to find their roots
because I mean what if
the world was a hell of a lot more beautiful.

And I think
that could be every smiling stranger
I've ever met.
Who has made me want to follow him
until the end
until the revolution is finally televised
and the revolution is us.

Wendy Noreña

Chemistry

my heart jumps out my throat when i see you.

i love it.
Hg is for mercury and it floods through my veins,
solid is the word, and the word is solid.

liquid gold rushes to the tip of my skin in the form of your palms

Ag is for silver, and it posts little beads of red across my wrist
si, aqui, here, now, i'm awake.

it's bitter, i guess. but more than anything i see you and the world
    is dizzy and you are so bright

sleep stakes me to the ground in the form of que.
if you can tell what i am feeling right now then i am doing this
    wrong.

porque?

that's also a good one. yo estoy contigo y tu conmigo. but that's not
    an answer. just the word(s).

solid is the word.

the only word i don't have.

House yard sidewalk four-lane-busy-road sidewalk yard house

Alone feels a bit like late Sunday mornings when the house is quiet and everyone has left for a dip to the lake and no one had the courage to wake you from your aggravated slumber. It also seems a bit like when you come home on Saturday night with a headache and without a few kisses that you left in the care of strangers with symmetrical faces and you just feel sick but you don't want to wake your mom up because she worked hard enough that day: money for alcohol. Alone is an elastic hair band when you need to keep vomiting of aggressive fear and also wide open doors when you're holding boxes on moving day: effortless coincidence will make life easier but someone wasn't there to lend their hands, murmur encouragement, or pick up that string of pride that keeps dragging itself through the dust. Some people say it's tracing the line between house-yard-sidewalk-and then onto street with the tip of a bicycle tire, breaking into fresh summer air with the yearn of sweat and pumping legs. And yet alone is being seven years old while you're still 8 and 9 and every age from then up until you become 20 or 30 and you realize all that time went by and there isn't a single memory that automatically comes up in your mind when the idea of a happy past comes back to harass as the ghost of your childhood. Alone becomes the emptiness of not knowing and the fullness of knowing too much when you can't speak of it and in that way alone does not exist. Alone wants to say a "lone," a loner, a person, a brother, a kinship never broken and when you walk the curb and cross that line of house, yard, sidewalk, four-lane-busy-road, sidewalk, yard, house you stop being alone. You become a neighbor.

#3

When I first saw the
Moon
Tumble out your mouth and
onto the shores
of my comprehension
I thought of you
as Venus bursting out
of conscious sea foam
(the gentle bubbles like possibilities)
and I admit I tried to cover you up
with an urgent gusto of innocence
wishing timidly to know you
just as the wind knows the
silhouette of your skin.

It happened thus:
you, me.
Room Moor,
Moored in place by
A faction of teenage soliders,
singing wayward songs for
round-about attention.
There was also,
perhaps an entourage of mine,
standing in the corner.

I was afraid to go alone.

A moment sprung open
like early March
so I spoke.
I looked back
to where dark clouds met
Dark dreams
nights when I couldn't sleep.
And then
Seeing the moon,
which resembled the
movement of your teeth
and quick flash of your tongue,
the words tumbling out like
waves
and Venus shouting her own name
I'd imagined the man in the moon
like a father of light,
who saw all and was all
led the stars to a solid armistice
Above earth's lanky shoulders
Saying, "watch me.
I am also the son (of earth, of stardust, of you)"

And I knew then connectivity,
And hope,

and a need choked the words out
to look for knowledge where
I'd never known it.

No one said anything.
The room sat on its haunches
Anchored to silence,
not towards sea.
Then
you said you saw him too.

Wendy Noreña

FreeLikeACagedBird

There's a free bird,
Somewhere.
Flying with an open sore smile,
And a chuckle of wind,
She is not me.

I sit,
Dead concrete,
Looking up.
You are the quick sand
worry.
Sucking softly,
against my grain,
With your heavy sense of
Ownership.
If only stones
Could be for more than throwing
If only they could fly
For longer than the second before they hit
Me in the knees.

I can succumb to the motion sickness,
Easy.
Well,
That is me and who better to fix

Or love
What I have done
Than me.
No one better.

You slander my ankles
With tears
And tell me not to go yet GO,
contradict yourself
but not me.
I'm stone, I'm arrow, I'm flock of bird,
I point in your direction.
I'm all yours.
Tell me what you want,
Please.

Could you let me be the free bird for once.

Wendy Noreña is a Colombian-American student, poet, performer, science fanatic and regular teenager. She was born in Medellin, Colombia and lived there until the age of three before moving with her parents to Atlanta, Georgia. She attends school at the Westminster Schools of Atlanta where she participates on the Student Diversity Leadership council and the Community Service Committee. She has spent the past year in France as a high school junior learning about French-European society and culture while enjoying the delicious pastries, taking advantage of the many travel opportunities France has to offer, and exploring environmental studies.

In her free time Wendy enjoys making art (in any medium), writing poetry and researching the various facets of the scientific world, as well as sharing animated conversation with fellow travelers and collaborating on community-impacting projects. This is her first time being published, but she hopes to continue writing and sharing her love of the power of words with young people.

Trence King

Among Crystals and Halcyon Descending Feathers

Standing in the midpoint of a room bordered by mirrors. From above, the divine feathers are descending to my level. The actions of a dream, seeing as though the roof above me had been turned into a path for falling beauty. Arrogance for this dream had shown me the likes of a pattern I call absolute. Absolute radiance from fire and heat I accepted. And who could conceptualize being burned at the event? If this place could ever be a retreat, I feel that I, and anyone could learn to grasp the helve of life's beauty and wonder more easily. This place harnessed angelic presence, and I felt true. True to the thought of dominance and success to say that anything shall be accomplished with effort. Non-hindering light whispered the truth and phenomenal ideals necessary for everything.

The Harbinger of Misfortune:
Gannon Unnamelle

At peace with miscalculations, the growth of misfortune is repressed. Is it wise to adapt to the potential of failure in each ounce of effort you give? Or is it wise to ignore the signs of useless energies? I only preach from my experience and well thought out logic given the filth and ignorance that some, perhaps you, possess. I had no intentions of breaking your hope. My theory is to lose your efforts to gain control of constant knowledge; this is of most importance in my beastly opinion.

But to many this logic might be......sad. However, sad is only an excuse the weak use as reasoning for being...defeated.

Guardian of the Embassy:
Chronological Foreshadowing

Over there, between laziness and the order, lies an individual test. The screams heard as we've walked by the alleyway, were not even an element of consciousness. Not even an instance of a thought to show concern. But the distressed young voice calling for help should have been enough for anyone to commit a good deed. Was it worth it to go home to that phone call we were in a hurry for? Not getting that job promotion put a stamp on the front page of our worst week. I'm sure the situation that was ignored wouldn't have prepared anyone for the negative news. But it would have for the decisions we will have to make in the future. If we can save someone, we must. It is the antidote to your sickness, for it is the antidote to mine.

The Red Insignia

How you get your point across seems to be troubling you. Your method of delivery leaves your listeners ears in great

malfunction

because of little sense your words make. And in your haste, you scramble your own thoughts in hopes that you didn't create a puzzle for your hearer. Are you a paradox or a contradiction? How horrible it is to be upset. Explaining yourself is the biggest obstacle in your life. Or it may not be in fact the smallest.... or biggest. Whether or not you lose or fail isn't the point. I mean to display the essence of failing itself in thought of not being one with confusion. But only I could possibly tell that I may or may not be indecisive, because you're not. You are not wrong in this because you understand that it could simply be right. Or maybe you've been wrong the whole time.

 My name is **Trence King**, and I aspire to be the creator of multiple sagas of sci-fi and suspense short stories and movies. My genre of writing tends to be vast including elements of drama, horror, love, and of course sci-fi. I would like for my work to be known and loved by people with multiple movie and story interests. I also write poetry about either personal belief, conceptualizations, or simply about something interesting. I also play guitar in a hardcore metal band called Dimensions. My inspiration for writing is the multiple elements of life and human culture. Some of the things we encounter in life are of glorious creation or of evil creation. And I find it interesting and fun to create stories and fictional worlds based off of our everyday experiences.

Aly

5:40

I walk
and it's black bleeding gold
egg yolk oozing from a wanna-be-sunset, smog-filled sky
and the red dawn turns to blue dusk if you stare long enough
and the wind doesn't nip at my neck
or bite my cheek but rather
kisses my nose and whispers
into my lashes—"it might be dark
but it's only 5:40. it might be cold
but you have a blanket knit from rain.
and sunset is just another lens
filter on this half-shaded world."

alliteration

i. She was a cirrus cloud, her body just grazing the stratosphere.

"The view's amazing up here," she would say, a smile flitting across her eyes. "You should come up once in a while."

Elevator cables have nasty habit of snapping near the top.

ii. She was a spiderweb, her fingers stretched as thin as her heart.

"That's the problem with being everywhere, you're always only halfway there," she would say, fingering her cotton candy hair.

Hitchhiking is always looked down upon.

iii. She was a snowstorm, her words stinging like hail.

"You know, the most beautiful dreams come out of nightmares," she would say, not even looking, "It's always dark right up 'till dawn."

But there are always days when the sun doesn't rise.

iv. She rose like Aphrodite, she fell like Hephaestus, and she died like Icarus, a dream slipping through her lips.

Triton

some people fall asleep
to the sounds of the ocean
the metronome of Poseidon
beating time like a clock

some people drift away
on waves of constant motion
the monotony of Neptune
pounding sand from rock

some people close their eyes
and absorb the commotion
of rolling swells
and within each dwells
a symphony,
a life

Silent City

i.
'o city splayed,
nude figure 'cross the land
does your breath grow heavy,
when weighed down by man?

ii.
o' city splattered,
paint stains your floor,
are your wooden bones battered?
your asphalt arms, sore?

iii.
o' city split,
have the maggots been killed?
the kingdom keeps crumbling
as the burnt blood spills.

iv.
o' city splintered,
as this night turns to day,
must the tides vanish?
does anything stay?

v.

o' city silent,
wind knocks at your door,
but no one can answer,
not anymore.

Aly's love of writing has a long history, stretching back to kindergarten, where she wrote her first fan fiction—an epic tale about Mickey Mouse saving Minnie Mouse from an earthquake. The book had been stapled on the wrong side, right instead of left, and half the letters were backwards. Luckily through experience, she has grown to be a much more confident writer. Growing up, she spent most of her time exploring imaginary realms with her friends, leading to the vivid imagination she has today which she expresses through her writing.

She lives with her family and her dog, both of which are major influences in her life. Aly draws most of her inspiration from everyday experiences, ranging from walks with her dog to conversations with her friends. But perhaps the greatest influence in Aly's life is the Internet, where she has grown as both a person and a writer.

Aside from writing, Aly enjoys reading, playing video games, playing the piano, taking walks with her dog, and watching television. She's always ready to jump into new experiences and is very excited to share her writing with you in this anthology.

Critical Reading Questions and Writing Exercises

These critical reading questions and writing exercises are designed to enable young readers to engage with and explore the literature of the young writers of this anthology. Each question or exercise includes a reference to one or more of the Common Core State Standards with which it aligns. A listing of those standards is included at the end of this section for reference purposes.

"Because the Crow Flew South"

1. How does the use of repetition and parallelism contribute to the meaning of the poem?
[CCSS-ELA-Literacy.RL.9-10.4, 11-12.4]

2. Write a letter or poem to a person you care about in which you express how the relationship between you and that person has developed over time.
[CCSS-ELA-Literarcy.W.9-10.4, 11-12.4]

"Obsessed"

1. What is the poem saying about gender roles and expectations? Consider what the narrator says explicitly and what she implies.
[CCSS-ELA-Literacy.RL.9-10.1, 11-12.1; W.9-10.1, 11-12.1]

2. Consider your perception of who you are versus the way others might see you; compare that to the narrator's experience as expressed in the poem.
[CCSS-ELA-Literarcy.W.9-10.2, 11-12.2]

"Things I Can Never Say to You"

1. How does the narrator's experience of the relationship differ from the way the other person experiences the relationship? [CCSS-ELA-Literacy.RL.9-10.2, 11-12.2]

2. Write a letter or poem to a person that you know in which you describe ways in which the two of you see something differently.
[CCSS-ELA-Literarcy.W.9-10.4, 11-12.4]

"Elephant"

1. Consider the narrator's comparison of herself to an elephant; how does this contribute to the central idea of the poem? [CCSS-ELA-Literacy.RL.9-10.2, 11-12.2]

2. Write a brief argument in which you support a claim as to whether or not the narrator's comparison of herself to an elephant effectively communicates her self-perception. Cite details from the poem.
[CCSS-ELA-Literarcy.W.9-10.1, 11-12.1]

"Backspace"

1. How does the author create a sense of mystery and tension within the story? Cite specific details from the story to support you analysis.
[CCSS-ELA-Literacy.RL.9-10.5, 11-12.5]

2. Consider the central metaphor of the cafe and how it relates to the theme of creativity. Write a short story in which you use your own metaphor to develop a theme about creativity.
[CCSS-ELA-Literarcy.W.9-10.3, 11-12.3; RL.9-10.2, 11-12.2]

"Reflections on a Palm Desert Dinner Party"

1. How does the poet influence your perception of the relationship between the wife and husband over the course of the poem? Cite details from the poem to support your analysis.
[CCSS-ELA-Literacy.RL.9-10.4, 11-12.4]

2. Write a brief argument as to whether or not the relationship between the two characters will last. Cite details from the poem to support your position.
[CCSS-ELA-Literarcy.W.9-10.1, 11-12.1]

"Cambodian Nights"

1. How does your perception of the daughter and her relationship with those around her develop over the course of the story? Cite details from the story to support your analysis.
[CCSS-ELA-Literacy.RL.9-10.3, 11-12.3]

2. Write a short story in which two characters fail to understand each other. Show this misunderstanding through the details and events of the story.
[CCSS-ELA-Literarcy.W.9-10.3, 11-12.3]

"The Fall"

1. How does the author structure the events of the story such that a feeling of tension is created? Cite details from the story to support your analysis.
[CCSS-ELA-Literacy.RL.9-10.5, 11-12.5]

2. Decide whether you think the incident between Tom and Elijah actually happened. Write an explanation of your conclusion, citing specific details from the story.
[CCSS-ELA-Literarcy.W.9-10.2, 11-12.2]

"9/21/12"

1. How would you describe the narrator's perception of his existence in your own words? Cite specific details from the poem. [CCSS-ELA-Literacy.RL.9-10.1, 11-12.1; W.9-10.1, 11-12.1]

2. Write a poem or short story that expresses how you experience your own life. If a poem, use a central metaphor to communicate your experience; if a short story, show your experience through the sequence of events. [CCSS-ELA-Literarcy.W.9-10.3, 11-12.3]

"Silence"

1. How does the poet use the concept of silence to develop the central theme of the poem? Cite details from the poem to support your analysis. [CCSS-ELA-Literacy.RL.9-10.2, 11-12.2]

2. Write a letter or a poem in which you which you ask someone to listen to you. Choose a central image or concept and develop your letter or poem using that image or concept to express your main idea. [CCSS-ELA-Literarcy.W.9-10.4, 11-12.4]

"Nothing"

1. The narrator states, "all of it means nothing." Do you think that is what she truly believes? Cite specific details to support your claim. [CCSS-ELA-Literacy.RL.9-10.1, 11-12.1; W.9-10.1, 11-12.1]

2. Write a short explanation of how the poet uses the opposite concepts of "nothing" and "everything" to develop the central meaning of the poem. [CCSS-ELA-Literarcy.W.9-10.2, 11-12.2]

"Walking Backwards"

1. How does the image of walking shape the central idea and meaning of the poem? Cite details from the poem to support your analysis.
[CCSS-ELA-Literacy.RL.9-10.2, 11-12.2]

2. Write a poem or short story in which you use an image or series of events associated with movement in order to convey your central meaning.
[CCSS-ELA-Literarcy.W.9-10.3, 11-12.3]

"When Reality Hits"

1. Do you agree with the way in which the narrator gave up? Justify your position.
[CCSS-ELA-Literacy.RL.9-10.1, 11-12.1; W.9-10.1, 11-12.1]

2. At the end of the poem, the narrator states, "That's why I gave up." In your own words and using details from the poem, explain what she means.
[CCSS-ELA-Literarcy.W.9-10.2, 11-12.2]

"Break the Glass"

1. The narrator is speaking to another person. Based on what the narrator says, how would you describe the character to whom she speaks?
[CCSS-ELA-Literacy.RL.9-10.3, 11-12.3]

2. Write a letter or a poem asking someone to do something for you. Use a central image to communicate your request.
[CCSS-ELA-Literarcy.W.9-10.4, 11-12.4]

"A Monster's Victory"

1. The narrator is describing another character. Based on what she says explicitly and what you can infer, how would you describe that other character?
[CCSS-ELA-Literacy.RL.9-10.1, 11-12.1]

2. Write an explanation of what the narrator means by "monster." Support your analysis with details from the poem.
[CCSS-ELA-Literarcy.W.9-10.2, 11-12.2; RL.9-10.4, 11-12.4]

"Helena the Poet"

1. How would you contrast Helena's vision of what she wants for her life with her mother's vision? Support your analysis with specific details from the story.
[CCSS-ELA-Literacy.RL.9-10.3, 9-10.1 11-12.3, 11-12.1]

2. Write the next scene in the story in which Helena reveals to her mother that she was the anonymous poet.
[CCSS-ELA-Literarcy.W.9-10.3, 11-12.3]

"Somethingdoesntfeelrightwheniwalkaroundhereanymore"

1. How does the poet's repetition of the phrase "if the world knew" contribute to the meaning of the poem?
[CCSS-ELA-Literacy.RL.9-10.4, 11-12.4]

2. The poem concludes with "the revolution is us." Analyze what is meant by that statement. Support your claims with details from the poem.
[CCSS-ELA-Literarcy.W.9-10.1, 11-12.1; RL.9-10.1, 11-12.1]

"Chemistry"

1. How does the poet use images related to chemistry to express the central idea of love?
[CCSS-ELA-Literacy.RL.9-10.2, 11-12.2]

2. Write an explanation of how the poet is exploiting a double meaning of the word "chemistry." Cite specific details from the poem.
[CCSS-ELA-Literarcy.W.9-10.2, 11-12.2]

"House yard sidewalk four-lane-busy-road sidewalk yard house"

1. The poet repeatedly uses the word "alone." What different perspectives on that word does she offer the reader?
[CCSS-ELA-Literacy.RL.9-10.4, 11-12.4]

2. Explain why the poem ends with the line, "You become a neighbor." Support your analysis with details from the poem.
[CCSS-ELA-Literarcy.W.9-10.1, 11-12.1; RL.9-10.1, 11-12.1]

"#3"

1. What is the significance of the moon as an image? How does it relate to the central idea and meaning of the poem?
[CCSS-ELA-Literacy.RL.9-10.2, 9-10.4, 11-12.2, 11-12.4]

2. The poem exploits an implicit association between the moon and the sea. There is a similar cultural association between the sun and growing plants. Write a poem or short story that makes use of that association.
[CCSS-ELA-Literarcy.W.9-10.3, 11-12.3]

"FreeLikeACagedBird"

1. The speaker of the poem is confused. What are the circumstances the poem describes that causes her confusion?
[CCSS-ELA-Literacy.RL.9-10.1, 11-12.1]

2. Write a letter or poem to someone who is causing you to feel confused. Use images or metaphors to communicate to that person why he or she is making you feel confused.
[CCSS-ELA-Literearcy.W.9-10.4, 11-12.4]

"Among Crystals and Halcyon Descending Feathers"

1. What are the ways in which the poem utilizes and develops a central allusion to the myth of Icarus? Cite details from the poem to support your analysis.
[CCSS-ELA-Literacy.RL.9-10.2, 11-12.2]

2. Choose a well known myth or story. Write a poem or short story that retells that myth or story in a different way.
[CCSS-ELA-Literearcy.W.9-10.3, 11-12.3]

"The Harbinger of Misfortune: Gannon Unnamelle"

1. What are the elements of the poem to contribute to its sense of tension and mystery? Provide specific examples from the story.
[CCSS-ELA-Literacy.RL.9-10.5, 11-12.5]

2. Write an explanation of why it is important to the meaning of the poem that the name of its central character, Gannon Unnamelle, is not a name you would encounter in real life.
[CCSS-ELA-Literearcy.W.9-10.2, 11-12.2]

"Guardian of the Embassy: Chronological Foreshadowing"

    1. What sickness is the poem addressing? Cite specific details to support your claim
[CCSS-ELA-Literacy.RL.9-10.1, 9-10.2 11-12.1, 11-12.2]

    2. Write a letter or poem to be published in the local newspaper in which you identify a social problem and present arguments as to why it needs to be addressed.
[CCSS-ELA-Literarcy.W.9-10.4, 11-12.4]

"The Red Insignia"

    1. How do the grammatical structures and phrases utilized by the poet underscore the theme of confusion and misunderstanding?
[CCSS-ELA-Literacy.RL.9-10.2, 11-12.2]

    2. Write your own poem about confusion or misunderstanding. Use grammar and phrases in ways that reinforce that theme.
[CCSS-ELA-Literarcy.W.9-10.3, 11-12.3]

"5:40"

    1. How is the use of color and visual imagery central to the meaning of the poem? Provide specific examples from the poem.
[CCSS-ELA-Literacy.RL.9-10.2, RL.9-10.4 11-12.2, 11-12.4]

    2. Write a justification as to why the time of 5:40 is essential to the meaning of the poem. Cite specific details from the poem to support your claim.
[CCSS-ELA-Literarcy.W.9-10.1, 11-12.1]

"alliteration"

1. What do the different images tell you about the central female character of the poem? Cite specific images in support of your claim.
[CCSS-ELA-Literacy.RL.9-10.3, 11-12.3]

2. Write a poem or short story that describes a character's personality and actions using weather-related images.
[CCSS-ELA-Literarcy.W.9-10.3, 11-12.3]

"Triton"

1. What aspects of the ocean does the poet use to develop the central idea of the poem?
[CCSS-ELA-Literacy.RL.9-10.4, 11-12.4]

2. Explain how the poem connects ocean related imagery to the concept of time. Support your analysis with specific details.
[CCSS-ELA-Literarcy.W.9-10.2, 9-12.1, 11-12.2, 11-12.1]

"Silent City"

1. What are the different images of the city that the poem creates in your mind?
[CCSS-ELA-Literacy.RL.9-10.2, 11-12.2]

2. Think of the city in which you live. Write a letter or poem to be published in the local paper that conveys how you see your city using vivid imagery.
[CCSS-ELA-Literarcy.W.9-10.3, 9-10.4, 11-12.3, 11-12.4]

Common Core State Standards, Reading: Literature

CCSS.ELA-Literacy.RL.9-10.1
Cite strong and thorough textual evidence to support analysis of what the text says explicitly as well as inferences drawn from the text.

CCSS.ELA-Literacy.RL.9-10.2
Determine a theme or central idea of a text and analyze in detail its development over the course of the text, including how it emerges and is shaped and refined by specific details; provide an objective summary of the text.

CCSS.ELA-Literacy.RL.9-10.3
Analyze how complex characters develop over the course of a text, interact with other characters, and advance the plot or develop the theme.

CCSS.ELA-Literacy.RL.9-10.4 Determine the meaning of words and phrases as they are used in the text, including figurative and connotative meanings; analyze the cumulative impact of specific word choices on meaning and tone.

CCSS.ELA-Literacy.RL.9-10.5 Analyze how an author's choices concerning how to structure a text, order events within it create such effects as mystery, tension, or surprise.

CCSS.ELA-Literacy.RL.11-12.1 Cite strong and thorough textual evidence to support analysis of what the text says explicitly as well as inferences drawn from the text, including determining where the text leaves matters uncertain.

CCSS.ELA-Literacy.RL.11-12.2 Determine two or more themes or central ideas of a text and analyze their development over the course of the text, including how they interact and build on one another to produce a complex account; provide an objective summary of the text.

CCSS.ELA-Literacy.RL.11-12.3 Analyze the impact of the author's choices regarding how to develop and relate elements of a story or drama.

CCSS.ELA-Literacy.RL.11-12.4 Determine the meaning of words and phrases as they are used in the text, including figurative and connotative meanings; analyze the impact of specific word choices on meaning and tone, including words with multiple meanings or language that is particularly fresh, engaging, or beautiful.

CCSS.ELA-Literacy.RL.11-12.5 Analyze how an author's choices concerning how to structure specific parts of a text contribute to its overall structure and meaning as well as its aesthetic impact.

CCSS.ELA-Literacy.RL.11-12.6 Analyze a case in which grasping a point of view requires distinguishing what is directly stated in a text from what is really meant.

Common Core State Standards, Writing

CCSS.ELA-Literacy.W.9-10.2 Write informative/explanatory texts to examine and convey complex ideas, concepts, and information clearly and accurately through the effective selection, organization, and analysis of content.

CCSS.ELA-Literacy.W.9-10.3 Write narratives to develop real or imagined experiences or events using effective technique, well-chosen details, and well-structured event sequences.

CCSS.ELA-Literacy.W.9-10.4 Produce clear and coherent writing in which the development, organization, and style are appropriate to task, purpose, and audience.

CCSS.ELA-Literacy.W.11-12.2 Write informative/explanatory texts to examine and convey complex ideas, concepts, and information clearly and accurately through the effective selection, organization, and analysis of content.

CCSS.ELA-Literacy.W.11-12.3 Write narratives to develop real or imagined experiences or events using effective technique, well-chosen details, and well-structured event sequences.

CCSS.ELA-Literacy.W.11-12.4 Produce clear and coherent writing in which the development, organization, and style are appropriate to task, purpose, and audience.

National Governors Association Center for Best Practices, Council of Chief State School Officers. *Common Core State Standards English Language Arts*. National Governors Association Center for Best Practices, Council of Chief State School Officers, Washington D.C. 2010

Permissions

Natalie Camrud: "Because the Crow Flew South." Copyright 2013 by Natalie Camrud. "Obsessed." Copyright 2013 by Natalie Camrud. "Things I Can Never Say to You." Copyright 2013 by Natalie Camrud. "Elephant." Copyright 2013 by Natalie Camrud. Printed by permission of the author.

Emily Glenn: "Backspace." Copyright 2013 by Emily Glenn. Printed by permission of the author.

Isabel DeBre: "Reflections on a Palm Desert Dinner Party." Copyright 2013 by Isabel DeBre. "Cambodian Nights." Copyright 2013 by Isabel DeBre. Printed by permission of the author.

Hayden Kinney: "The Fall." Copyright 2013 by Hayden Kinney. "9/21/12." Copyright 2013 by Hayden Kinney. Printed by permission of the author.

Briana Richardson: "Silence." Copyright 2013 by Briana Richardson. "Nothing." Copyright 2013 by Briana Richardson. "Walking Backwards." Copyright 2013 by Briana Richardson. "When Reality Hits." Copyright 2013 by Briana Richardson. "Break the Glass." Copyright 2013 by Briana Richardson. "A Monster's Victory." Copyright 2013 by Briana Richardson. Printed by permission of the author.

Cristianna Cummings: "Helena the Poet." Copyright 2013 by Cristianna Cummings. Printed by permission of the author.

Wendy Noreña: "Somethingdoesntfeelrightwheniwalkaround-hereanymore." Copyright 2013 by Wendy Noreña. "Chemistry." Copyright 2013 by Wendy Noreña. "House yard sidewalk four-lane-busy-road sidewalk yard house." Copyright 2013 by Wendy

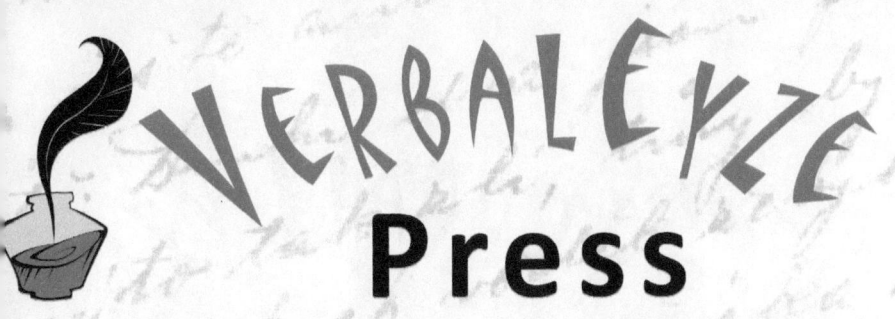

VERBALEYZE Press

Empowering young writers to say, **"I am my scholarship!"**

Open call for submissions to the *Young Writers Anthology!*

See your work in print!

Become a published writer!

Earn royalites that can help
you pay for college!s

VerbalEyze Press is accepting submissions from young adult writers,
ages 13 to 22, in any of the following genres:

- poetry
- short story
- songwriting
- playwriting
- graphic novel
- creative non-fiction

For submission details, visit
www.verbaleyze.org

VerbalEyze serves to foster, promote and support the development
and professional growth of emerging young writers.

VerbalEyze
Writers Cooperative

VerbalEyze is a nonprofit organization whose mission is to foster, promote and support the development and professional growth of emerging young writers.

The *Young Writers Anthology* is published as a service of VerbalEyze in furtherance of its goal to provide young writers with access to publishing opportunities that they otherwise would not have.

Fifty percent of the proceeds received from the sale of the *Young Writers Anthology* are paid to the authors in the form of scholarships to help them advance in their post-secondary education.

For more information about VerbalEyze and how you can become involved in its work with young writers, visit

www.verbaleyze.org.